TEAM WORK

A picture essay about crews and teams at work

Photographs and text by George Ancona

Thomas Y. Crowell   New York

Library of Congress Cataloging in Publication Data
Ancona, George.
    Team work.

    Summary: An essay in words and photographs that shows
how individuals in various crews, teams, and work gangs
depend on one another to get a job done.
    1. Work groups—Juvenile literature.   2. Teamwork
(Sports)—Juvenile literature.   [1. Work groups.
2. Teamwork (Sports)   3. Work.   4. Sports]   I. Title.
HD66.A52 1983   658.3′128   82-45579
ISBN 0-690-04247-7
ISBN 0-690-04248-5 (lib. bdg.)

10 9 8 7 6 5 4 3 2 1
First Edition

TEAM WORK

Jobs get done and goals are reached by organizing a variety of people with differing skills into a crew, team, or work gang. As part of a crew, each member is needed to do his or her part at just the right moment. In some crews, the jobs are specialized, each member having a particular skill to contribute. In others, roles are interchangeable, and each person knows the work of the other. In a good crew, each individual becomes sensitive to the needs of his or her crewmates, and when one has a problem, a partner is there to help. Mutual respect and friendships grow out of working together—along with the good feelings that come from a job well done.

This book explores a variety of crews and teams, looking at what each person does and how it fits together with the work of the group.

CONTENTS

MOUNTAIN CLIMBERS

Two people tied to each other with a rope and harness—that's the only safe way to climb a mountain. In addition to the right clothes, shoes, and a rack of chocks and carabiners, what is needed is trust in the skill and good sense of one's partner. While scaling a sheer wall of rock a climber is on his own— the rope in his partner's hands becomes a lifeline.

A climb begins with each climber tying one end of the climbing rope to his or

her harness with a double figure-eight knot. The lead climber moves ahead while her partner stays behind to belay her—tied to a tree or rock, he slowly lets out the rope. Inching along, she wedges a chock into a crevice and snaps on a carabiner to hold the rope. This is her protection. Should she slip, he could stop her fall by tightening his grip on the rope. Reaching the first ledge, she now belays for her partner.

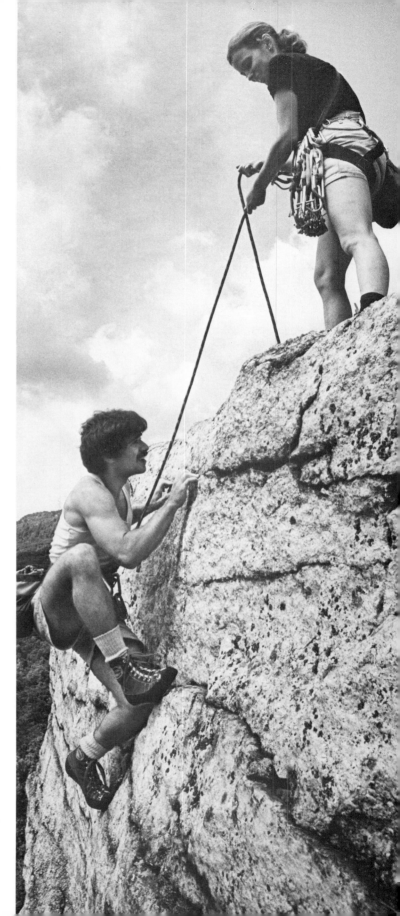

Now the other climber leads. His partner belays from the ledge below. The climber carries a pouch filled with chalk dust. The chalk keeps his hands dry, giving him a surer grip on the rock. He too protects himself by placing chocks and carabiners as he moves on.

Having traversed the overhang, the lead climber then belays his partner from above. This also gives him a chance to rest.

As she traverses, she "cleans the protection" from the cliff face by removing the chocks and carabiners—nothing is left behind.

In this leapfrog fashion they move up the mountain. At the top they enjoy the exhilaration of having reached their goal.

ROUGHNECKS
(Drilling Crew)

Drilling for oil and gas takes place all over the world, on land, in marshes, and at sea. The people who work these derricks, or drilling rigs, are called roughnecks. Drilling goes on twenty-four hours a day. Four-person crews come on every eight hours. The *tool pusher* is the person who supervises the drilling operation and is on call for all three shifts.

A *driller* is in charge of the crew for his own shift. He operates the control box, controls the weight on the drill bit, and runs the hoisting and drilling equipment.

The *derrickman* is the crew member who works high up on the derrick when drill pipe is raised out of the hole. He is also in charge of the engines, pumps, and air pressure for the drilling string, the name given the entire length of drill pipe in the hole. With a cathead and rope, he lifts new pipe sections to the rig floor.

The *chain hand* throws the "spinning chain" around the pipe to connect or disconnect drill-pipe sections.

The *corner hand* works with the chain hand. Both are considered *floor hands*. During a shift, crew members will sometimes switch jobs.

This land rig is drilling for gas. As the drill bit bites through the many layers of sand, rock, and shale, thirty-foot lengths of pipe are added to the drilling string to push the bit still deeper.

When the kelly, the forty-foot steel section attached to top end of the drilling string, reaches the derrick floor, it is time to add another pipe. At the control box the driller stops the drill while the derrickman bleeds the air pressure off the standpipe. This is the pressure that forces fluids down to the drill bit to carry away the loose debris. The kelly is raised slightly, so the floor hand can drop the tapered slips into the rotary table. These wedge the string in place in the hole while the new length of pipe is being added.

Breakout tongs are attached to the kelly to disconnect it from the pipe.

The floor hands disconnect the kelly, swing it over, and lower it into the "rathole," where it will wait until needed again.

The blocks are disconnected from the kelly with a long rod, and elevators are latched on to the new drill pipe.

The new pipe is raised over the end of the old one and connected. The slips are removed, and the new pipe is lowered into the hole.

Again the slips are dropped into the rotary table to hold the new pipe. Now the elevators are used to bring the kelly over to the new pipe. The spinning chain is thrown in order to spin up, or connect, the kelly to the pipe.

Once the slips are removed, the drill string will begin another thirty-foot trip into the earth.

As the derrickman hoists with the cathead, two of the crew move a fresh pipe from the storage rack to the rig to be ready for the next connection.

NURSING TEAM

The day-to-day care of patients in a hospital requires people with a variety of skills. In many hospitals this care is provided by nursing teams. In this manner the patient has the constant attention of a nurse and nurse's aides. As in a family, each member of the team helps the others to attend to their patients' physical and emotional needs.

The *head nurse* manages the staff of one floor of the hospital. She confers with the doctors, orders supplies, organizes the nursing teams, and assigns the teams to the patients they will be caring for. At the beginning of each shift, she meets with the teams to discuss the condition of the patients and what their needs are for that shift.

The *assistant head nurse*, also one of the team leaders, will fill in for the head nurse in her absence.

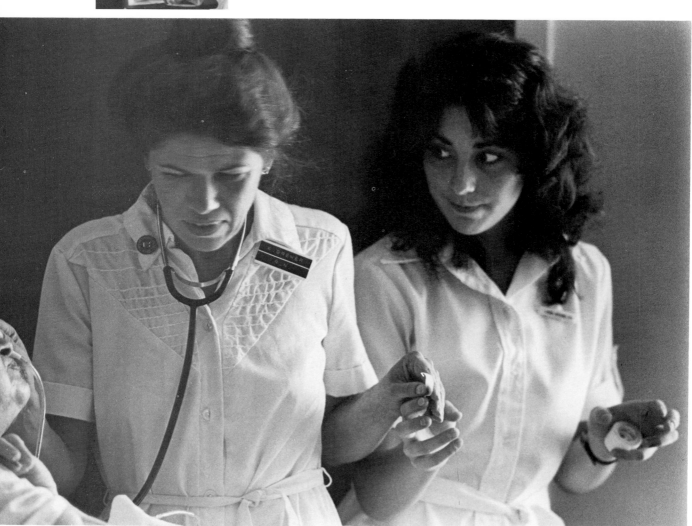

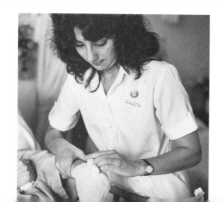

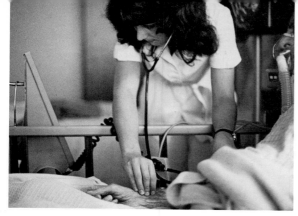

The *team leaders* are nurses who provide their patients with all the nursing procedures they need. They change bandages, take temperatures, blood pressures, and pulses, obtain specimens, and administer what treatments are required. They will often help each other with complicated procedures and treatments. Patients who spend long days and weeks in bed must be turned every two hours to keep them from getting bedsores. Often it takes two people, a nurse and a nurse's aide, to do this.

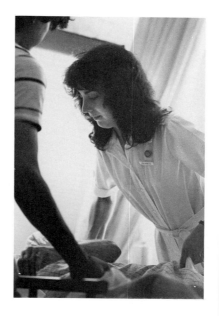

The *senior nurse's aide* has the most experience of the aides on the floor. He or she will teach the new aides what has to be done and how to do it.

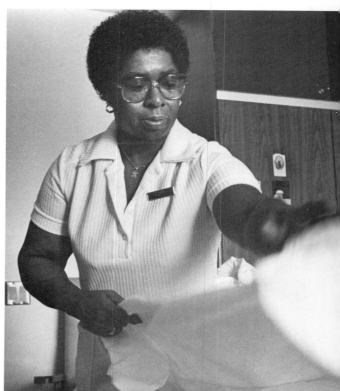

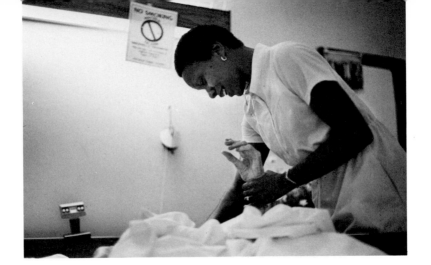

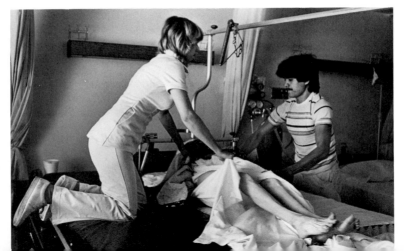

Nurse's aides do the jobs that allow nurses more time to do the medical treatments their patients need. The aides transfer patients from beds to wheelchairs and stretchers. They take them to other floors for X-rays, physical therapy, or hairdressing, or outside for some air. They wash those that can't do it for themselves. They make beds and empty bedpans. During mealtimes, they pass out the food trays and feed those who need their help. They stay in constant touch with their patients, notifying the nurse of any problem. Their cheer and comfort are part of the treatment.

The *medication nurse* takes her cart of medicines around to each patient. She prepares and dispenses the doctors' prescriptions along with some kind words. It is this support and encouragement that are an important part of the healing profession. They make the stay in the hospital a little more bearable for the patient.

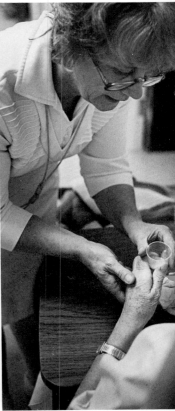

FILM CREW

Movies are made by people with specialized skills working together as a team. A film crew can be made up of many people or just a few, depending on the kind of film being produced. Regardless of its size, the crew's job is to record the action in moving pictures and to record the sound on tape. This is what films are made of.

The *producer* is responsible for raising the money to pay for the production of the film. She hires the director and supervises the arrangements for travel, salaries, supplies, food, and lodging. She also guides the film through all the processes to the finish.

The *director* has the overall responsibility for the crew and the making of the film. She decides what to shoot, where to shoot it, and what the general look or style will be. She will direct people to produce what is in her imagination and what she wants the movie to communicate.

The *cameraperson*, working with the director, selects the rest of the crew. He photographs the action. By using lights, color filters, and movement, he will create the mood that the director is trying to achieve.

The *soundperson* records the sound as the cameraperson shoots. With headphones, she monitors the sounds as they are recorded on a portable tape recorder. Before the camera is turned off, the soundperson flashes a number, which the cameraperson shoots. This number identifies the recorded sound with the action just shot. In this way the precise sound take can be found on the tape and combined with the correct picture take.

The *gaffer* lights the scene the way the cameraperson wants it. Using a light meter, the gaffer makes sure that there is enough light on the scene for it to be well photographed.

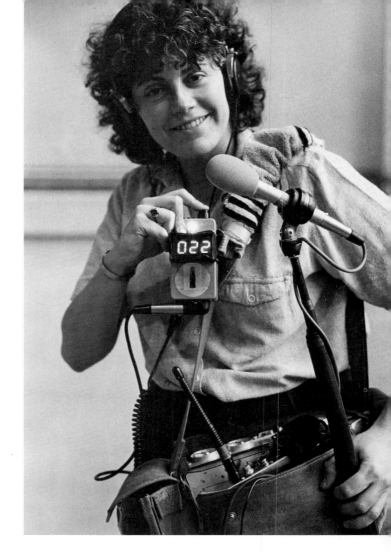

This crew is shooting a television documentary film about children who study dance. In a documentary, the people in the film are not told what to do or say. Actions are shot as they happen. The cameraperson carries the camera, instead of using a tripod, so he can move quickly and follow the movements of the children. Meanwhile the director watches for other actions that may be important for the story.

The soundperson moves with the camera, recording the sounds. By using a microphone on a pole, she can bring it close to the subject to get the best sound while still keeping the mike out of the camera's frame.

Later, more people take over the making of the film. Film labs develop the pictures. An editor selects and edits out unwanted takes and puts the pictures together with the sound. A composer writes music and conducts musicians in a recording session. Sound engineers blend the sounds onto one sound track. Finally, the laboratory will make the finished print we will see on television.

PIT CREW

Stock car races are won by a finely engineered auto, a daring driver, and a skilled pit crew. During a grueling 500-mile race, the driver will have to make several pit stops. Tires are changed, the gas tank filled, adjustments made, and the driver is given a drink...all with split-second timing.

This team races two cars. The pit crew is in constant touch with the drivers by two-way radio. When a pit stop is called, the *crew chief* will signal the crew to get ready by holding up his fingers to indicate how many laps to go. By radio, he counts off the laps to the driver. Each man grabs the equipment he needs: gas can, jack, speed wrench, windshield wiper, scrub brush, or drink.

On the last lap, one man holds up a sign board with the car's number. This is a target for the driver, who roars into the pit at almost 150 miles per hour.

As the car stops, six men leap over the wall. The *front wheel changer* drops to his knees and, using a high-speed wrench, begins to loosen the lug nuts.

Another man, the *rear wheel changer*, loosens the nuts on his wheel. Between the two, the *jack man* slides a lightweight jack under the car's chassis and pumps the handle as fast as he can. One side of the car is lifted off the ground. He then moves on to help the front wheel man.

The *tire man*, with a 75-pound racing
slick under each arm, moves in quickly
and places one wheel alongside each
wheel changer. Before the race, lug
nuts were cemented on the wheel to
speed up the change. In his pocket, the
tire man carries extra lug nuts to
replace any that are knocked off when
the wheel is shoved into place. If neces-
sary he goes on to make chassis
adjustments.

As the wheels are changed, the *gas man* shoves the "dry break" nozzle of the 90-pound gas can into the filler neck of the car's gas tank. Each can

holds 11 gallons. The car takes 22 gallons—
two canfuls—of special high-octane
racing fuel. Meanwhile, up front, the
driver is handed his drink on a pole.

Refueling is speeded up and hazardous gas spills are avoided by not using a gas-tank cap. The tank opens when the nozzle of the gas can is pushed in and closes when it is removed. Alongside the gas man another crew member holds the gas overflow can. When the tank is full, gas spills into the catch can from an overflow pipe in the rear of the car.

It takes about seven seconds to remove the wheels and empty the first can of gas. As the nuts are being tightened on the fresh wheels, the second gas can is being emptied.

When the gas man sees gas spilling from the overflow pipe he yells to the jack man to drop the car as he pulls out the can. The driver is given the "go" signal, and he roars off to join the race.

FASHION DESIGN TEAM

The clothes we wear are the result of the work of thousands of people in the fashion industry. Styles change every season. New colors, new fabrics, new shapes, and new ideas all excite people into buying the new season's fashions.

The process begins with a fashion design team producing a sample of a new garment. This one-of-a-kind sample will be shown to the buyers for department stores and dress shops. If they like it, they will order many garments in a variety of colors and sizes. Now the factories can begin to manufacture enough garments to fill the orders.

The *designer* comes up with the sketches of new ideas. Next to the drawings, he staples swatches of the fabrics to be used in the garments.

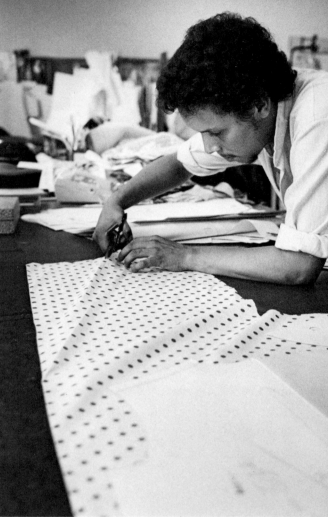

The *pattern maker* designs the pattern based on the designer's drawing. After sketching out the many parts of the garment, she cuts them out of heavy paper. These are the plans for the construction of the sample.

Now the *cutter* takes over. He traces the pattern onto the fabric selected by the designer. The grain and the most economical use of the fabric must be considered. He then cuts out all the pieces needed to make the garment.

In this particular studio two *sample hands* work at sewing the cutout pieces of fabric into the finished sample garment. Each can produce an entire sample alone, or they can work together on one garment.

When the sample is finished and pressed, the garment is put on a dress form or a live model. The designer looks it over and may make some changes. The pattern maker may have to cut a new pattern, or the sample hand make a minor alteration. Once the designer approves, the new garment is ready to be shown to store buyers.

SAILING CREW

A sailboat moves by catching the wind in its sails. To change the boat's direction, the crew adjusts the sails, sometimes changing the sails entirely in order to get the most speed from the boat. In a race, the crew must move swiftly and together as a unit.

On a twenty-four-foot racing sloop the crew can consist of:

The *helmsman*, who with one hand on the tiller steers the boat and with the other handles the mainsheet (the rope attached to the boom), controlling the position of the mainsail.

The *winch grinder*, or *jib man*, who sits forward of the helmsman, controls the headsail (jib, genoa, or spinnaker), the sail used forward of the mainsail. He adjusts, or trims, the sail by using the ropes attached to it (halyard and sheet). He tightens or loosens the sheet by using a winch, which helps him hold on to it.

headsail (genoa)

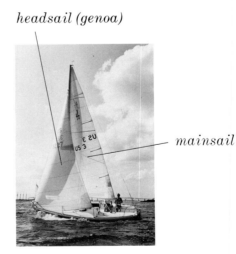

mainsail

The *middleman* stands in the open gangway and takes the fresh sails out of the cabin, attaching them to the sheets and halyards for hoisting. He then gathers in the original sail and stores it below. He is also needed to help reposition sails when changing direction.

The *forward-deck man*, or *bowman*, helps in raising or lowering headsails. When the boat is flying the spinnaker, he helps control the sail with a spinnaker pole. Since sails cut down visibility for the helmsman, the bowman also acts as lookout and informs the helmsman of the set of the sails and the direction of the boat.

spinnaker

When changing the direction of the boat, or tacking, the helmsman calls out "Ready about" to warn the crew. He then calls out "Hard-a-lee" and pushes the tiller to head the boat into the wind. This empties the sails. As the mainsail boom swings over to the other side of the boat, the jib man loosens the jib sheet. The crew scrambles under the

boom while moving the headsail to the other side. The jib man tightens the opposite sheet. The sails fill with air, the boat heels over, and the crew members settle down into their new positions on the other side as the boat heads into a new direction.

starboard tack

When the wind is behind the boat the crew hoists the spinnaker. This huge colorful sail pulls the boat along at a very fast speed.

port tack

ACKNOWLEDGMENTS

I should like to thank the people who helped make this book possible by generously sharing their time and knowledge with me.

Mountain Climbers
Patricia Lanzetta
Brett Wolf

Jon Ross, guide

Roughnecks (Drilling Crew)
Jim Kittle, tool pusher
Justin J. Day, driller
Richard Nicola, derrickman
Robert V. Laugh, chain hand
William D. Watts, corner hand

Brad Liggett, drilling superintendent,
    Union Drilling, Inc.

Nursing Team
Rita Fowler RN, head nurse
Linda Benton RN, assistant head nurse
Kathy Deeds RN, team leader
Louisa Watson RN, team leader
Retha Harris, senior nurse's aide
Genevieve Kiely, nurse's aide
Delores Williams, nurse's aide
Rosalind Whelan, nurse's aide
Noel Abordo, nurse's aide
Barbara Calise RN, medication nurse

Rockland County (N.Y.) Health Center

Film Crew
Muffie Meyer, producer
Ellen Hovde, director
Tom McDonough, cameraperson
Samantha Heilweil, soundperson
Meredith Birdsall, gaffer

Middlemarch Films

Pit Crew
Wade Thornburg, crew chief, tire man
Jimmy Martin, team manager (windshield)
Horst Fischer, stick man
Johnny Cline, jack man
Brandy Cox, tire man
Steve Hmiel, tire man
David Lovendahl, tire man
John Morgan, helper
Mike Hart, board man
Bill Helms, gas man
Wayne Dalton, gas man
Carl Fortune, gas man

Maurice Petty, chief,
    Petty Enterprises

Fashion Design Team
Gregory Odea, designer
Sabina Illes, pattern maker
Rafael Ortiz, cutter
Marianela Picard, sample hand
Suzy Kang, sample hand

Sailing Crew
Drake Johnstone, helmsman
Billy Drewes, jib man
Jeff Johnstone, middleman
Stuart Johnstone, bowman

J World

Gail Rosovsky who did the research for the book and *Rosemary Russo* who typed the manuscript.

Thank you all!